THE WAY OF THE
URBAN SAMURAI

THE WAY OF THE
URBAN SAMURAI

The laundry as perceived by Mrs. Hokusai

THE WAY OF THE
URBAN SAMURAI

As revealed by

Kasumi

Charles E. Tuttle Company, Inc.
Boston • Rutland, Vermont • Tokyo

First published in the United States in 1992 by the
Charles E. Tuttle Company, Inc. of Rutland, Vermont & Tokyo, Japan,
with editorial offices at 77 Central Street, Boston, Massachusetts 02109

Cover design and illustrations by Kasumi.

CIP data available from the Library of Congress.

LCCN 92-19192

ISBN 0-8048-1817-7

PRINTED IN THE UNITED STATES ON ACID-FREE PAPER

To Kitao,
son of the Urban Samurai

Contents

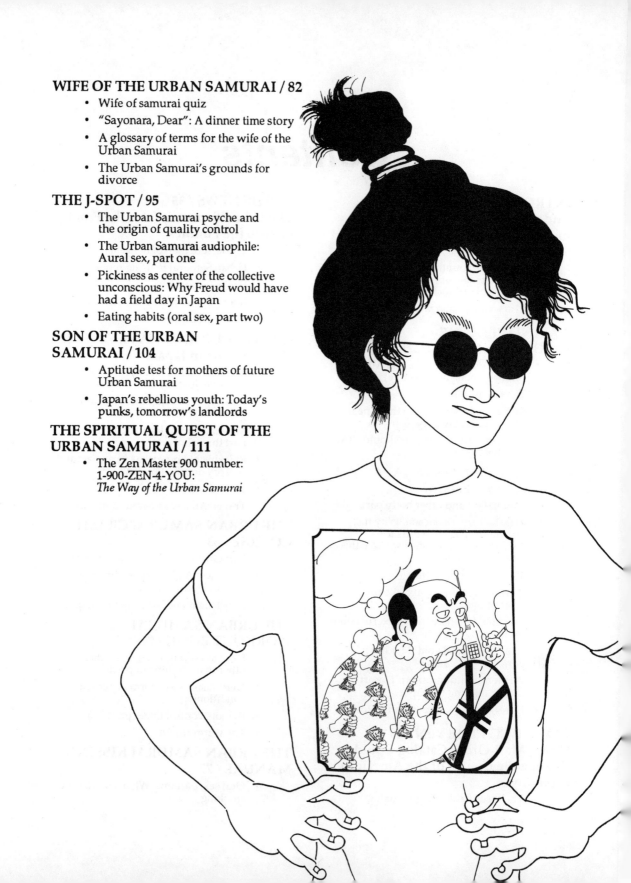

Introduction:
Understanding the Prodigy
of the Industrialized World,
the Urban Samurai

O.K. So you've read *Japan As Number One,* you take karate lessons and eat tofu, and you still can't figure out why Japan is fast becoming the world's dominant financial power. Mainlining soy sauce doesn't help either, because the real force behind that phenomenon called Japan is the Japanese male himself, the Urban Samurai. You Westerners will penetrate the innermost secrets of Japanese success only when you understand this master of cleverness and inscrutability. In order to understand him you must examine his surroundings, his daily life, his company, his TV shows. What does he do with his money besides buying hair emollients and American Treasury bills? Is "the one-minute Samurai" a brilliant theory of Japanese business management, or does it refer to his sex-life?

There has been a veritable explosion of misinformation disseminated about the Urban Samurai in the past few years — everything from misinformed, blockbuster novels to misinformed, insipid TV shows. All are total fabrications written and produced by non-Japanese. After all, how would you feel about a TV program broadcast in Japan — written by a non-English-speaking Japanese whose entire foreign experience consisted of 35 minutes in Topeka — that portrayed every single American man, woman, and child as a red-necked, welfare-dependent gangster, and have the entire population of Japan believing every word?

The time has come to clear up misunderstandings about the Urban Samurai, which are just about the only things Westerners have about him. I offer you the ultimate, information-packed, compendium of enlightenment on the subject — from an insider's point of view and understanding. Whether you are doing business with, marrying, being bought out by, or just plain curious about the Urban Samurai, this is the only book you will ever need.

You have probably been fooled by the outward appearance of the Urban Samurai, replete with three-piece business suit, Hermes attaché case, and Rolex watch: just another businessman rushing to his next meeting. But the fact is, beneath this familiar façade is a being so alien you would have to travel to another galaxy — or at least Yuba City — to find anyone more diametrically opposed to Western man.

Unlike Western man, for example, the Urban Samurai has no belief in a single All-Powerful Deity, except himself. His mental energies are directed instead toward an unending search for beauty and perfection within the realm of everyday life. The Urban Samurai is not concerned with such trivialities as upward mobility, status seeking, or a good back hand. He is into bigger concepts such as peace, serenity, and lowering the capital gains tax.

2

The Urban Samurai is so culturally advanced and possesses such finely honed instincts that he has negotiated agreements with three major American companies by the time he enters kindergarten and has diversified into corporations on three continents before he reaches puberty. His pre-historic ancestors were soaking in hot tubs before Los Angeles was invented, and were eating high-tech designer foods before Western man could handle a spoon.

With the yen rate soaring, sushi bars putting delicatessens into extinction, and Fortune 500 companies issuing quarterly reports in Japanese, it is not just helpful — *but a matter of survival* — to understand that prodigy of the industrialized world, the Urban Samurai.

A check-out counter of the Edo period

JAPAN, THE COUNTRY

The True Meaning of Overcrowding and the Cultural Origins of Gridlock

The Urban Samurai lives in what Americans would consider the most crowded nation on earth. Since 98 percent of the Japanese islands are filled with cash card machines, computer stores, and other uninhabitable areas, the population density of livable parts of Japan is the equivalent of half the entire inhabitants of lower Manhattan stuffed into a two-bedroom apartment. Try to imagine every person living in a 75-unit condominium complex attempting to use the bathroom at the same time — *your* bathroom.

Mt. Fuji as viewed from Mr. Tanaka's 80th floor apartment

Try to imagine the chaos that occurs when 12 million people try to cross the same intersection simultaneously. Try to imagine waking up one morning to find that an 80-story chrome-and-acrylic office building has been erected in your child's backyard sandbox. Imagine 8 million people in front of you at the checkout counter every time you go shopping. Try to imagine living with your in-laws. And that's just the suburbs.

THE WEATHER AND WHAT TO DO ABOUT IT

Westerners think of Japanese weather as calm breezes filled with the aroma of cherry blossoms all year-round, but in truth it is a disaster. At this very moment, Japanese scientists are working feverishly to do something about it.

As nasty as the weather may be, however, it does not alter the relentless path of the Urban Samurai. For example, during the rainy season it rains 24 hours a day for a solid month. A typical Westerner would stay home, watch soap operas all day, fondle his Jarvik-7 artificial heart, and feel sorry for himself. But does this miserable weather daunt the Urban Samurai? Absolutely not. He takes out 12 new patents on automatic, battery-operated umbrellas, has them manufactured in Taiwan and mass-marketed in the U.S.A., diversifies into satellite controlled bicycle brakes and microwave ovens, and spends the rest of his years retired in Albuquerque, much of which he now owns.

Does it matter to him that the heat and humidity of the summer are enough to poach eggs or that the winters are so cold that freeze-dried coffee was invented by having a cup of real coffee sit around his house for a couple of minutes in February? And how about typhoons and earthquakes? Does the Urban Samurai get depressed just because at any minute his entire country could be sucked off the face of the Pacific Ocean? Of course not, but he does get upset over a 0.0001 decibel variation in the performance of his stereo speakers.

So how does the Urban Samurai — crammed into a little tiny country where it rains all the time, where a pound of beef can cost $300, and where a golf club membership can cost $2.7 million — manage to get along with all his fellow Japanese?

THE SHOGUN TOKUGAWA AND MBO
(MANAGEMENT-BY-OBJECTIVE)

Developing a concept of the history of Japan by reading *Shogun* or watching "Ohara" reruns is like trying to learn Western civilization by reading *Archie* comic books and eating at McDonald's. The most important forces in the development of modern Japanese society are not the founding of Sony and the invention of the vending machine, but the administrative genius of the 17th-century shogun, Ieyasu Tokugawa.

Being an astute businessman as well as a powerful warrior, when the shogun Ieyasu Tokugawa gained power, instead of moving his headquarters to the traditional seat of authority at Kyoto, he established himself at what is now Tokyo, predicting that land values there would skyrocket in just a matter of centuries.

During the 200-year Tokugawa shogunate — a time when the well-known Japanese concept of extremely long-term strategic business planning originated — the country was transformed from an untidy gaggle of bickering factions (your typical contentious agrarian society) into a highly organized feudal system of rigid hierarchy, eventually leading to what now is known as "lifetime employment." Tokugawa's use of decapitation as a punishment for minor production slip-ups is considered to be the core of modern "management-by-objective" philosophy. The Urban Samurai knows this as "management-by-removing-objects."

THE RICE IS IN THE MAIL

The main crop of the Japanese agricultural society was rice, even before Chico-san rice cakes. It was not only the staple of the Japanese diet, but the method of tax payment cruelly imposed by the shogunate. (Economic historians have pointed out the remarkable similarity of that process to the IRS long form). It was also a real pain in the honorable gluteus maximus to produce: The main element ensuring a successful crop was back-breaking, labor-intensive cooperation. Rice production was impossible to undertake singlehandedly, so one simply had to get along with one's neighbors, even if that meant going to more barbeques, craft-fairs, and piano recitals than you thought humanly possible.

Precise timing was also of the essence; the rice had to be harvested at the exact moment it was ready. You couldn't stay home to let the plumber in or even wait for your fingernails to dry. "The rice is in the mail" did not cut it with the local *daimyo.*

Thus, despite the Westerner's romantic vision of the Japanese as swash-buckling swordsmen, more accurate is the image of a throng of hungry farmers, working with frantic relentlessness under the threatening edge of a sword. They toiled to get that rice planted, grown, and harvested before the whole field was vacuumed away by a typhoon, swallowed up by an earthquake, incinerated by marauding bad guys, or recycled into a Taco Bell restaurant.

REMAINING A STRANGER TO THOSE NEAR YOU — PROBABLY VERY NEAR YOU

Generations of cooperative rice production made the Japanese group-oriented even before Ban Roll-On or Tic Tac breath mints. But regardless of the reasons, whether tilling the soil together, living in intolerably close quarters, or just thinking that being polite and wearing navy-blue school uniforms are fun, the key to the Urban Samurai's value system is social harmony, or *wa*.

The total commitment to cooperation and mutual understanding is why decisions are made by consensus and not by any individual. The delivery date of 68,000 Isuzu flat-bed trailer trucks is placidly implied; a woman is granted permission from her husband, her in-laws, and a team of doctors to give birth; the work force of a company jumps out of the plant's 10th-floor windows en masse when sales are sluggish.

ETIQUETTE

Should You or Shouldn't You Bow Before Sex?

Etiquette in Japan is not something used only at luncheons with the emperor or when you're asking for a raise. It is a way of life — perhaps *the* way of life — and it means knowing, or at least trying to figure out, one's exact position in relation to others. The quest to pinpoint one's precise role in the hierarchy of Japanese society is what is referred to as *knowing one's proper station*. This is why there are so many people on the street constantly consulting those little wallet-sized subway maps and scratching their heads.

The quest to pinpoint one's precise role in the hierarchy of Japanese society is what is referred to as *knowing one's proper station*. This is why there are so many people on the street constantly consulting those little wallet-sized subway maps and scratching their heads.

YOU ARE HERE

10

The young show deference to the old, women to men, men to creditors. This respect is manifested in the arrangement of seating, particularly at office parties, noodle restaurants, on laps, and during prime time. Moreover, individuals held in reverence always get the first choice of desserts. The chairman of the board is always entitled to the last slice of chocolate torte with whipped cream, while the first vice-president must settle for a runny egg custard. If there are disagreements or questions as to who deserves what, a coin is tossed. In the case of a draw, a general walk-out occurs, the workers go on strike, and the business goes bankrupt. Thus, knowing one's proper position is essential to successfully running a large company.

Even in the realm of sexual relations, protocol takes precedence over pleasure. The question is not whether one should bow before sex or not, but exactly how low: Bowing levels, which are calculated to correspond to the Nikkei index, are listed daily in all major financial publications.

However, except for elevators — where all passengers face front, don surgical masks, and keep their hands neatly folded in front of them — all rules of etiquette are disregarded the minute one enters a train or any other moving vehicle.

Commuting . . .

. . . in Total Harmony

Communication in Japan: Say What, Tanaka-san?

SAVING FACE AND OTHER BODY PARTS

Obviously the Japanese just *hate* being embarrassed. They are always leery of precarious positions so that social faux pas — such as sweating, ordering something other than noodles for lunch, or leaving the soap wet after use — are to be avoided in the first place. This cultural imperative is called *saving face*.

Face is not something that can be squirreled away in a safe-deposit box to be extracted and worn on a rainy day, although it would be nice to go out one day as Greta Garbo and as a sperm whale the next. If this were possible it would not be unusual to see 30 or 40 people on any given day looking just like Dan Quayle or Madonna.

Saving face is a way of life in Japan. The Urban Samurai must constantly be on the lookout for situations that lead to embarrassing or compromising predicaments. To take chances is to risk appearing foolish, so any kind of new or different behavior must be done within the realm of convention. Saving face is the reason that divorce and crime rates are lower in Japan than in most other countries. It is the reason gifts are never opened in the presence of the donor, and the reason a worker will never tell his superior that his fly is open.

For example, your typical subway flasher will carry out his transaction in the most businesslike manner possible. His attire will always be a conservatively tailored business suit topped by a slate gray London Fog raincoat. His inside jacket pocket will contain Ichigo Teshigahara's important volume, *Proper Comportment of Perverts in All Situations*. He will be impeccably groomed and will bow sharply before he performs his ministrations. Upon completion, he will hand the recipient of his attentions a 1000-yen note in an envelope specially manufactured for the purpose, bow again, and — when he reaches his subway stop — take his leave.

TRUE FEELINGS vs. FAÇADE

***Why the Japanese have 123 words for "excuse me"
but none for "take this job and shove it"***

In face-to-face confrontations, outward self-control takes precedence over inner feelings.

The following are examples of the concept of *honne-tatemae* (true feelings vs. façade).

Two businessmen meet at the office:

> Mr. Yasushi Dewlap *thinks*: Hey, Lardbreath! How's that monster of an old maid daughter of yours?
>
> And *says*: Ah, Plaque-san, how is your lovely daughter?
>
> Mr. Takeshi Plaque *thinks*: May the sweat of a thousand sumo wrestlers infest your armpits.
>
> And *says*: Quite fine, but she certainly pales in comparison to your two charming girls.

Two housewives meet on the street:

> Mrs. Noriko Normal *thinks*: Oh no, that hippo again. Every time I set foot out of my house I have the rotten luck to run into her.
>
> And *says*: Oh! You're going for a walk.
>
> Mrs. Satoko Saccharine *thinks*: What a moron. No, I'm conducting the Berlin Philharmonic.
>
> And *says*: Oh, yes, there's a special at the market today.

Husband and wife:

Of course, once married, the concept of *honne-tatemae* applies only to the wife.

> Wife: A cat has four legs.
>
> Husband: Right, you stupid jerk. Did you say you had a kindergarten diploma?

However . . .

> Husband: A cat has four legs.
>
> Wife: Oh honorable husband, how profound and wise are your insights.

Using a Third-Party Negotiator:

Often, to avoid direct confrontation in delicate transactions, a go-between is engaged. The neutral party carefully steers around squeamish issues and can even terminate negotiations without either faction losing face. For instance, a business transaction . . .

Mr. Yin: Close but no cigar, Cockroach Tongue.

Intermediary: He finds your offer very kind.

Mr. Yang: That ten-legged frogmutant would sell his own ugly mother — if anybody would have her — to improve his business.

Intermediary: Mr. Yang is flattered. He also extends greeting to your charming mother.

Or the same technique can be applied to marriage brokering:

Mr. Fishheads: Tell crater-face that I've seen better looking broads as stand-ins for Godzilla.

Intermediary: Mr. Fishheads is charmed by your subtle good looks.

Miss Ricecakes: Inform four-eyes that his retarded mother should wash his underwear occasionally.

Intermediary: Miss Ricecakes has remarked on the good taste of your attire.

TELEPHONE COMPORTMENT

Ruling out his conduct on rush-hour trains and at home, the Urban Samurai is the most polite being on earth. Telephone comportment is no exception and has been brought to a fine art.

Hello?

Hello, this is Aoki.

Ah, yes, thank you.

Thank you for your hospitality the other day.

Oh, no, no. Don't mention it.

Thank you. Fine weather we're having, isn't it?

Yes, quite nice.

By the way, is my older brother there now?

Huh? Who? Excuse me?

Oh! I'm sorry! I seem to have dialed the wrong number, but very pleasant chatting with you.

Hmmmm, I suppose so . . .

Says: Yes, well, I'm terribly sorry to trouble you. Good-bye.

Thinks: Too bad your brain operation was a failure, you maggot.

Says: That's quite all right. Good-bye now.

Thinks: Perform a reproductive function with yourself using your nose.

18

WHAT TO DO WHEN YOU CAN'T ANSWER YOUR PHONE

While *hai* can portray an intricately subtle range of meanings, verbal transmission of a basic idea takes 30 to 40 percent longer to say in Japanese than in a Western language. For example, most of us are really tired of those annoyingly cute telephone answering messages and would gladly forego listening to the entire first movement of Beethoven's Ninth Symphony or a 15 minute Jay Leno telephone joke monologue for a simple "Here's the tone: gimme your message." In Japan, where *hold* is a four-letter word, this would be an enormous breach of etiquette. A Japanese answering machine would contain a message that coaxes or suggests, not demands a reply.

Greetings, most respected and honorable caller. Shamefacedly, the dwellers of the Sato household do not have the high honor of receiving your gracious call personally. It is with bowed head and lowered eyes that we humbly beg you to leave your esteemed name, exalted telephone number and sublime message on our lowly answering machine after the tone has disturbed your serene contemplation. Please excuse this disrespect, forgive our rude and brash ways, and allow us to have the privilege of returning your revered call.

19

ESSENTIAL JAPANESE IN FIVE EXCRUCIATING MINUTES

Unbeknownst to travelers, businessmen, and scholars, who have all long held that the Japanese language is so intricate and cryptic that only the Japanese mind can master it, five minutes is all it takes to become fluent. The fact is, despite the thousands and thousands of words made up by those indecipherable pictographs of which Japanese consists, there are only five essential words: *suru, hai, domo, sumimasen,* and *ah.* Like the Urban Samurai, himself, these five words have no clear meaning, but depend on the circumstance, context, and nuances of the speaker to clarify them. If pronounced correctly, you can travel, do business, or even live in Japan just speaking five words and not one native will ever suspect that you were not born in his country.

The first, *suru,* is the verb "to do," which is tacked on to virtually any word to turn that word into a verb. For example, *sports* (pronounced "supotsu") *suru* means "to do sports." After the disasterous Japanese state dinner at which President George Bush emptied the contents of his stomach onto the lap of the Prime Minister, *Bush suru* has come to mean "to throw up."

The most complex of the aforementioned words is *hai,* since its meanings are innumerable. Its pronunciation is not like the "hi" of "hi, ya'll." It is shorter, as if your air supply had been cut off half-way through. Imagine starting to say "hi" and in the midst of speaking someone sneaks up behind you and, with one smart blow between the shoulder blades, beats the wind out of you with a two-by-four.

Hai can, of course, mean "yes," but more often than not, it is simply an acknowledgment of comprehension, an outward sign that you are listening to the speaker, or an indication that the listener hasn't been taken off his life-support system.

For example:

"Eat cockroach stew and die." *Hai.*

"That was some tart I saw your old man with last night." *Hai.*

"Whoa, Thunder-Thighs, you be havin' some bad food attacks lately." *Hai.*

In groups of twos or threes, *hai* can be used to indicate an elevation of aggravation, annoyance, or downright anger, usually said by a wife to her husband. *Hai* can mean "here" as in "here is your tea." *Haihai* means the same thing but is used when the husband, who has been sitting in front of the TV for about three hours without moving, has demanded his tea at the very moment the four-year-old has removed six weeks' accumulation of leftovers from the refrigerator out onto the floor and is skating across the room on two slabs of tofu. If four or more *hai*'s have been said, the wife has already filed for divorce. Difficult business negotiations, life-long relationships, and entire seasons of television programming are often carried out with this one word.

The pronunciation of *domo* will present no problems at all if you can remember to make the first syllable longer than the second and if you don't have a severe head cold. Most text books translate this as "thank you," but it is a rather superficial interpretation of a very complex part of the Japanese vocabulary. *Domo* can mean, "and how," or "how about that," "indeed," or "oh, it's you again." It may be used in conjunction with *hai* or *ah* as in *hai domo*, said after being informed by your stockbroker that you are now financially ruined. *Ah, domo*, with the first syllable stretched out, means "Well, fancy meeting you here," or "Well, I'll be; look who's on the phone." The word *domo* is always used, accompanied by short bows and nervous head scratching, when two acquaintances run into each other at a sexual aids supply store.

Sumimasen, pronounced phonetically ("sue-me-mah-sen"), is an extremely important word because it is used for apologizing, which the Japanese are always doing. For example, it can mean "excuse me" or "sorry," as in "Excuse me for puncturing your left ventricle with my scalpel." It may be an apology for a meager meal, as in "Please pardon the worthless crudity of this pheasant under glass." In this case the head must be lowered as well. After this is said, the husband uses the same word to apologize for the clumsiness and stupidity of his wife.

Given the fact that obscurity is not just tolerated but actually cultivated in the Japanese language, it makes sense that a nonword is an essential component of Japanese speech. *Ah* is not quite a word but more than a sound, and it can mean just about anything by the way it is pronounced. It is the correct response to the statement, "You're fired." If released with the proper amount of force, *ah* would also be the appropriate interjection offered when a fast-moving 16-ounce hammer has had occasion to come in contact with your thumb instead of the nail toward which it was aimed. *Ah* would also be the fitting rejoinder when you come home from work and find your wife, your mistress, and both of their attorneys in the living room throwing darts at your picture. *Ah* can conveniently be turned into an interrogative by changing the pronunciation to *eh* as in "Eh? The rent on this airless rat trap is $4000 a month?"

THE MEANINGFUL VOID

Making It Perfectly Unclear

No discussion of the Japanese language would be complete without talking about silence. The Japanese are very fond of voids, also referred to as *meaningful voids*. You have probably seen those nice Japanese scrolls with lots of uncluttered space — a common example of the meaningful void. The space left empty on a plate of sushi does not imply stinginess. It is purposely left that way for another kind of artistic meaningful void, namely, the void left in your wallet after paying for it.

The area between the ears of Japanese popular singers and career politicians are meaning*less* voids and are in the same classification as the void emitted by Madison Avenue, conversations with the in-laws, and the stupifying blather that goes on at singles mixers.

Pregnant pauses in conversations do not mean that either party has fallen asleep; these silences are meaningful voids as well, and indicate that thinking, admiring the surroundings, or enjoying the effects of a hallucinogenic drug is taking place. This principle is prevalent in communication and is why the Urban Samurai is such an expert at reading between the lines.

For example:

> Hiroyuki Preen: Ah, domo.
>
> Kenji Quadruped: Ah, dooomodomo.
>
> Preen: Ah, domo.
>
> (Both men suck wind through half-closed mouths while bowing and mumbling a few more "domos".)

Instead of wasting valuable business time discussing the weather, the drinking that went on last night, and the intrinsic meaning of Kantian philosophy, these two men, like true Urban Samurai, get right down to the essence of the conversation. Indeed, a person who possesses the gift of gab is looked down upon and is thought to exist outside the sublime sphere of human understanding. Such a person would find more appropriate employment as a stand-up comic in a cheap night club than as a master of tea ceremony.

WRITTEN COMMUNICATION

The Art of Saying Nothing on Paper

Written as well as spoken communication should have that undercurrent of unstated sentiment, and business letters are an art form all to themselves. Not only is extreme etiquette in order, but the written word must always be presented aesthetically, encompassing the principles of the meaningful void.

In the most astutely composed documents, inscrutability counts as much as neatness; in other words, you should make it impossible to decipher the real motive and intent. When writing to a superior, or someone who thinks he is — even though you think he has the mentality of a pit bull — it is best to avoid mention of his name. In the most important cases, such as a letter to Michael Jackson, Queen Elizabeth, or your financial planner, the address should be left out as well, since it would be offensive to make them think their position and stature were not known to the entire world. The following is an example of the deliberate use of blank space to accentuate meaning:

October 33, 1948
From His Exalted* Honor's humble servant

*When writing to one's lawyer or therapist the word "almighty" should be substituted for "exalted."

HARA-GEI

Nonverbal Communication

An even more subtle form of communication — that which uses no words at all — is referred to as *hara-gei*, or the art of the belly. Of course, Westerners have "gut feeling," but this purely animal instinct is good only for that split second before your house is about to be vacuumed up by a tornado, your wife hands you the divorce papers, or you are handed a pink slip at the office. *Hara-gei* is a much more delicate ability. This unique skill — being able to express oneself without the use of words, and the capability to read such sublime transmissions — is why one can observe two or more Japanese men standing around not saying anything, but all nodding their heads in agreement.

24

In business negotiations, this translates into a silent battle of wills; the total silence around the conference table is the businessmen's way of feeling one another out. Each team is trying to convince the other that theirs is stronger; or perhaps they are all trying to come to an agreement, through nonverbal means, about where to order out for lunch. This ability, of course, takes time, and like any other skill — nuclear physics or brain surgery, for example — *hara-gei* takes practice. When operating in the realm of nonverbal communication, one must learn to develop and refine those facial expressions which best transmit responsiveness and inscrutability at the same time.

Gone With the Yen:
How a Mail-Order Catalog
Could Change the Course
of the American Economy

With his wallet jam-packed with credit cards, and an insatiable appetite for new products, the Urban Samurai has even surpassed the consumption-crazed Westerner in spending extravagance. The goods for which he goes deepest into debt are those originating in the West but which have been modified and perfected until they are clearly out of his price-range — everything from ball-point pens to superconductivity quantum interference devices.

Even though you Westerners may seem happy buying used yard tools and discounted seconds, if you wish to gain a deeper understanding of the Urban Samurai you must develop the use of his technique of selective assimilation. This is a brilliant economic theory, devised in post-war Japan by a team of politicians and business executives, in which consumer goods from another culture are used in order to learn from and eventually overtake the economy of that culture. You can start by ordering from *The Inscrutable Image Catalog*, the ultimate catalog of products on the cutting edge of Japanese consumption. Now for the first time available in an English language edition, *The Inscrutable Image Catalog* includes items that have been carefully selected and tailored for Western use. Using those valuable and serviceable products that the Urban Samurai uses will facilitate familiarity with him and help you on your path to enlightened economic superiority.

THE INSCRUTABLE IMAGE CATALOG

Eatman. Don't say "fast-food," say "FAX FOOD!" This is the amazing new generation of portable lunch boxes. Just connect this hand-held microwave infrared communicator to your Holofax EP 280 Interface, put in your order for lunch, and within seconds, anything from chicken teriyaki to cheese blintzes will be ready to eat. If you order now, a beautiful bamboo-patterned traditional Japanese 18-piece place setting for one is yours free of charge. If you should for any reason decide to return "Eatman" within 90 days of purchase, you may keep the rice bowl and little parasol — with our compliments!

System 105. The ultimate in precision Japanese calculators. Small and compact, it relieves your desk of unnecessary clutter. The beads, which respond to a flick of the fingers, slide smoothly along ultra-slim bamboo cylinders encased in a handsome warm teak-finish frame. This attractive unit blends with any decor and comes complete with a 4,000-year-old instruction manual in Chinese.

Holofax EP 280. Don't just fax your messages, *Holofax* them! Don't your important messages deserve more than a flat piece of paper? With the Holofax EP 280 you can actually send a three-dimensional representative of your company — not an animated or scanned version, but a holographic image of a living, breathing person. Bill collecting was never this easy!!

NEW! NEW! NEW! Our "naughty" version of the Holofax: the HOLOMATE 4-FUN . . . an all new way to say "Let's Fax!!!" (Customers over 21 only!)

29

NaviGuider. Are you sick of crossing the street in downtown Manhattan and realizing when you've reached the other side that you're in Teaneck? Savvy Tokyoites have been using for years what the rest of the world is just now discovering — the NaviGuider. This is the prototype of those glowing green navigational screens appearing on dashboards throughout the world. This simple device, which resembles an automobile's rear-view mirror when clipped onto the user's ear, calculates the shortest distance between two locations and displays a concise set of directions to minimize those aggravating and painful free-for-alls on city streets and subway platforms. A super-deluxe model — the NaviGuider DX — spews out instructions constructed from a database that contains the location of every sidewalk, pre-kindergarten cram school, BMW dealership, and sushi bar within a ten-mile radius.

Programmable Personal RoboWife. Watch your computer come to life with YOKO, the servant in a new generation of programmable robots designed especially for the home and hard labor. She stands a full 4 feet 10 inches, weighs only 90 pounds, and with the flick of a switch awaits your command. Simply by uttering a single word, her sophisticated circuitry will respond with precision and total reverence.

She will not only solve your math problems, serve and flatter the guests, and diaper the baby, but will also serve as a high-speed food *and* word processor. She can chop, slice, puree, dice, julienne, and spell-check and never tire or wear out. She will greet you at the door, hand you your martini, and apologize profusely. This incredible robot, available only through *The Inscrutable Image Catalog*, comes complete with an irrevocable lifetime Shinto wedding ceremony certificate.

Shogun Mark III. The ultimate in luxury cars, designed with the refinement of the past and the technology of the future, this vehicle provides everything for the Urban Samurai who must spend a great deal of time on the road. Priced at only $485,000, this limited-edition automotive phenomenon is just the answer to the demands of the budget-minded samurai personal injury lawyer, plastic surgeon, or corporate raider on the go: 0 to 60 in 3.8 seconds, top speed of 185 miles per hour, and a hefty 300 horsepower engine. For those who actually get *out* of the parking lot, its state-of-the-art air filtration system makes driving through the heaviest smog in Tokyo or even Orange County seem like a stroll on a mountain path. In addition, if you should be stuck in gridlock for more than eight hours at a time, a delicious bowl of steaming hot Chinese noodles will be automatically dispensed from the fully computerized glove compartment. Please state preference for soy sauce or chicken flavor. Elegantly simple, yet functional wood, paper, and tatami construction in the highest tradition of taste and flavor; standard equipment includes quadraphonic *koto* music, a beautiful flower arrangement on the dashboard, and built-in FARM (fax and radio modem) equipment. If you act now, a superlatively crafted pair of fuzzy dice will be yours at no extra cost. The deluxe export model, equipped with bullet-proof glass in all windows and rifle scopes, is now available in Los Angeles.

The Airmover Portable Hand-held Fan. This is the smallest personal air conditioner yet. Whisper-quiet, it is powered by radically new bioenergy, and will run in your home, office, on the train, or while waiting nervously during an IRS audit — anywhere. It's so simple to run that even telephone solicitors and insurance salesmen can operate it with minimal instruction. In its closed position this amazing device takes up no more room than a couple of pencils. Hold the fan while it is fully extended and feel that aerodynamic design go to work.

Geta-Walkers. Get ready, get set, Geta-Walkers! This brilliant Japanese design in footwear magically reapplies the impact of the hard ground to all parts of your body, thus turning a simple stroll into an exciting and stimulating experience. These fantastic clogs in authentic wood tone even let you walk through puddles without getting your feet wet. One size fits most.

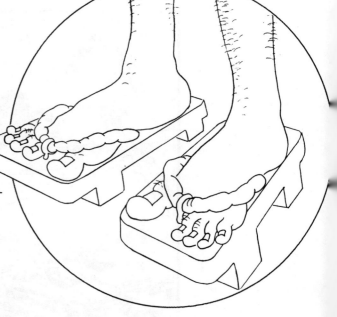

TeaMaster. Remember that bitter yet elegant brew drunk on the steps of the Heian-Jingu Shrine in Kyoto? Duplicate that ethereal flavor with our compact TeaMaster tea set and enjoy an authentic Japanese tea ceremony in the privacy of your own home. The set includes bamboo whisk, real tea-ceremony tea, measuring spoon, two 350-year-old cups, and a 93-year-old Japanese tea ceremony instructor.

32

Businessman's Survival Kit. Manufactured exclusively for I.I.C.'s readers doing business in Japan, this carefully chosen set of essentials will ensure that your next sale, merger, or takeover will be a success. The B.S. Kit includes business cards printed in Japanese; smile mouth insert, eyelid proppers, and a package of amphetamines to allow you to appear happy and alert — even after that sleepless 15-hour plane ride over; a dozen disposable self-adhesive three-piece navy blue business suits; our famous patented slip-on digital bower which instantly senses the level and frequency of bowing. Invisible when worn under clothing, it automatically bends you into the correct position when the need arises. And for those of you who never seem to know what to do with your *hands* when bowing, three cartons of cigarettes.

Samurai Stamina Set. Here is a complex series of weights, pulleys, and restraints that make all but the simplest tasks nearly impossible and excruciatingly painful. Even scratching your head will bring tears to your eyes. Put the "he" back in he-man and train in the way of the ancient Japanese warrior. Price includes the book *Samurai Coming of Age*, hospitalization policy, and permission slip to be filled out by your mother.

Executive Chopsticks. These are truly the Rolls Royce of eating utensils. Imagine the awe and envy on the faces of your business colleagues when you nonchalantly draw these burnished-aluminum chopsticks out of their ultrachrome carrying case with tough zennite handles. Makes eating an experience out of *The Tale of Genji*. Comes with instruction booklet and two months supply of stain remover.

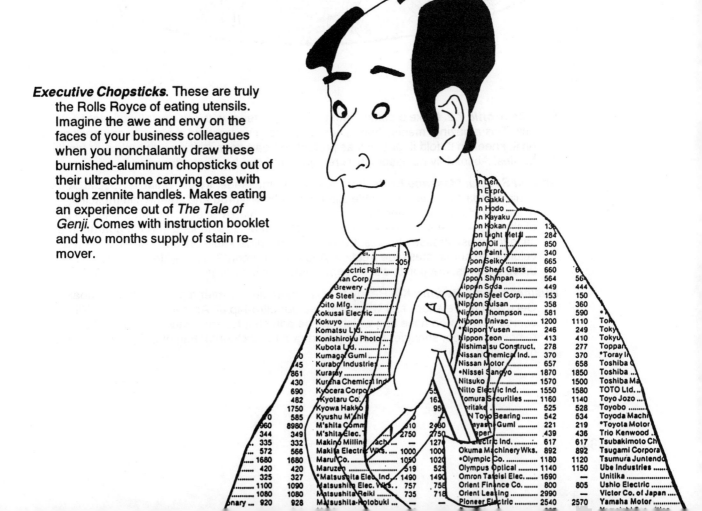

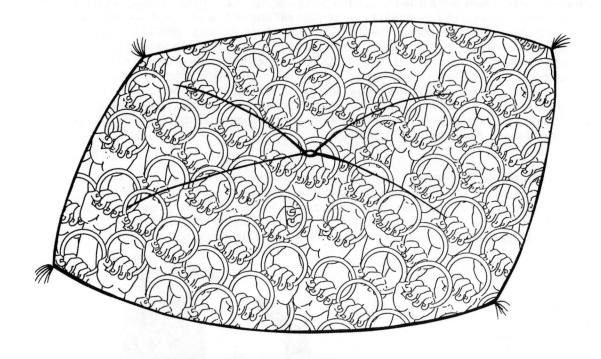

Ultra Zentronic 7.2. Make a commitment to your posterior with our multi-functional seating unit. This amazing, medically-engineered device can be used in virtually any position: sit on it, kneel on it, fold it, or use it as protective head gear during earthquakes or family tussles. Absolutely no assembly is required and can be stacked.

Shiatzu Special Massage Units. For the ultimate massage, try our Shiatzu Special. A pair of high-impact rubber retractable slip-on thumbs will prod and soothe stiff muscles, relieve pinched nerves and frazzled spirits. Our Shiatzu Special II comes with two pairs of slip-ons — one smooth rubber and the other a unique nubbed surface guaranteed to calm the most stressed bodies. Included in our remarkable price for either set is a ten-volume Japanese massage treatise. And if you purchase now, a life-size map of the 2,382 acupressure points will be sent to you free of charge.

Businessman's Reentry Kit. Ready to kiss American soil after a grueling trip to Japan? Get over culture shock fast when you use our ultra-hip all-American collection. Kit comes with clip-on nose ring which can be adjusted for ear; detachable ponytail; removable tatoo; shoulder holster (squirt-gun not included); bag of Doritos and 12-pack of chewing gum.

In the News:
The Urban Samurai,
from the Front Page
to the Funnies

The Western media have done an excellent job of portraying the extremities of the Japanese citizenry: for example, founders of multi-billion yen companies, noodle-shop owners who purchase original Van Gogh paintings, and deranged weirdoes who eat underwear. Tune in to any Japanese news program and you would think that all Westerners are differently sized, intellectually challenged, and alternatively motivated (fat, stupid, and lazy). All major Western news sources consistently manage to overlook some of the most important people and features of the Japanese press. Here are some of them.

THE LEISURE MAN OF THE YEAR

While it may appear to a Westerner that the only leisure activities in which an Urban Samurai takes part are practicing his golf swing on the station platform, decomposing in front of the television, smiling excessively for no reason at all, and making major scientific breakthroughs, the Urban Samurai is a veritable walking encyclopedia of fun things to do. Mr. R. Sato of North Eel prefecture and devotee of the game of pachinko was recently named Japan's Leisure Man of the Year and appeared on "The Importance of Fun in Modern Society," a five-minute monthly talk show hosted by Professor Daizo Amino of Keisei University's Department of Psychopathology.

Mr. Sato, sporting his official Pachinko Players International Association pin on the lapel of a natty three-piece navy blue polyester leisure suit, arrived punctually at the studio. Despite a severe hearing loss, "an occupational hazard of the game," he joked cavalierly, he proceeded to extol the virtues of the game for the 30 seconds that remained of the program after commercial announcements.

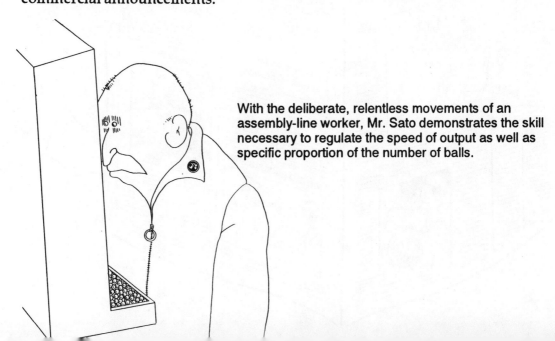

With the deliberate, relentless movements of an assembly-line worker, Mr. Sato demonstrates the skill necessary to regulate the speed of output as well as specific proportion of the number of balls.

URBAN SAMURAI HOUSING REPORT

The crushing crowdedness of the land of the Urban Samurai is causing a severe housing shortage, a condition not helped by the fact that a square foot of land in downtown Tokyo costs more than an entire city block in Manhattan. Up until now, the only remedy has been to live in intolerably small living quarters or to crash with the in-laws. Recently, however, Chicken-Wing Housing Corp. has developed the latest in living techniques through which a spacious, completely furnished ten room apartment can be stuffed into a four-and-a-half tatami-mat cubicle. It is called the drawer-pull apartment: one merely pulls the desired module out of the wall. Kitchen, dining-room, living-room, bedroom, bath, and S-M entertainment center can all be had at the tug of a handle. An exquisitely appointed model apartment can now be seen in the ever-growing Tofu Heights, between the Swimming Squid Cement Contracting Supply Company and Ernie's Beverage Center, on the second floor of the Ninja-noodle.

Of course, not to be outdone, in nearby East Radish the newest in accommodations for the happy twosome can be found at the Golden Condom Love Capsule. By discreetly slipping in the proper amount of money (or a Hanky-panky credit card) for the desired time allotment, a small compartment slides out into the darkened hallway. Upon entering (and ducking the heads, since there is only a one-meter clearance), the whole mechanism glides back into the wall. When the time is up the participants are automatically ejaculated back into the hallway. The newest model, The Safe Sex Capsule, which comes equipped with interactive virtual reality, is perfect for you health-conscious folks or for those individuals who just couldn't find a date for Saturday night.

But the need for space grows and grows. The final solution — barring the removal of the entire Japanese population to Outer Mongolia or Cleveland Heights — as researched by the Japanese Aeronautics and Space Administration, is the brilliant development of the weightless condominium. In this unit, every cubic millimeter of space can be put to use. Shelves become a thing of the past, and sleeping mats and their bulky storage problems are rendered obsolete since sleeping on air is like, well, sleeping on air.

The researchers have also designed the weightless love-hotel where, according to the tired but smiling research scientists, anything goes. The only snag in their experiments so far has been figuring out how to keep that little foil-wrapped packet from floating away out of reach.

BOOKS FOR SURVIVAL

MEGAZEN by L. Ron Takahashi, Rising Yen Publishing Co., 340 pages, $45,000, embossed leather edition.

Problems such as: how to sell four million cars in a country that already resembles a parking lot crammed full of late-model cars; how to manage a company whose number of workers is larger than the population of an average American metropolitan area; how to give a delivery date through means of transcendental meditation; and how to get through a Japanese business luncheon without getting soy sauce on your tie, are all succinctly solved in financial and managerial wizard L. Ron Takahashi's latest best-seller, *Megazen*. Dubbed "the business-man's bible" by *Monopoly Magazine*, this volume is causing a revolution in the Western business world.

Quoting heavily from the famous Tokugawa-era treatise, *Hara-kiri*, (recently published into English as *Suicide and Fiscal Accountability* by Rising Yen Publishing Co. in its extremely popular "Do It Yourself" series), Takahashi explains the simplicity with which Western companies can transform themselves from behemoth, money-losing dinosaurs into behemoth, money-making dinosaurs.

Using colorful, easy-to-follow charts and diagrams, Takahashi, a former Zen master and now president of Takahashi Management Consulting and Market Research Associates, shows how a Japanese salary man entering a company is the equivalent of a European entering a religious order. To explain a few highlights of his astoundingly brilliant theory, a worker is convinced, through a series of ten-day workshops, that misery is his fate and all man's pursuits are mere figments of the imagination. Next, Takahashi outlines a course of study for a 14-year-long crash course that teaches the worker to recite the Gettysburg Address using only the words *yes* and *no*.

A Megazen company realizes that a worker is not a mere "Nine-to-five drone" in a company, he is a 24-hour-a-day one. The Megazen company worker is not only imbued with the spirit of his company, he has actually found salvation in the absolute loyalty and devotion to his boss. He possesses the courage to sacrifice his life on the production line and his pride at the company picnic. He has attained emotional cruise control.

The core of the relationship in a Megazen company is "total, unconditional self-renunciation on the part of the worker to his company." The worker lives each day as if it were his last, and is a paragon of self-restraint and austerity — characteristics developed by years of eating at the company canteen.

The former holy man goes on to assert that if all company members were put on a nourishing diet of rice, fish, pickles, and miso soup; if it were rendered impossible for worker and high-level executive alike to transfer to another company without losing all seniority; and if a simple lobotomy were performed on each employee in a specially set-up government-approved out-patient clinic, a perfect balance between self, society, and company could be struck and history would be a thing of the past.

Next week **BOOKS FOR SURVIVAL** will interview Bagodonuts Kilokeester, last year's all-Japan sumo champion, whose book *Life in the Fat Lane* was on the *Tokyo Times* bestseller list for three minutes.

Life in the Fat Lane

INTERVIEW WITH THE CHAIRMAN

MAGURO SASHIMI, chairman of the Flapping Heron Pickled Plum Corporation, the largest manufacturer of pickled plums in Japan, granted *Monopoly Magazine* an exclusive interview last May. The history-making event took place in Mr. Sashimi's Kawasaki City retreat overlooking a panoramic view of the Love-of-Country Boiler Works and Pig-Iron Smelting Foundry Co., Ltd. Flapping Heron's chief since 1899, Maguro Sashimi is credited with developing snap-action, spring-operated chopsticks.

The large tatami room in which the interview was conducted was the quintessence of Japanese understatement. The only furnishings were a low table with silk-covered seating cushions on either side, an exquisite flower arrangement in a small alcove in one corner of the room and a buxom blonde draped over an iridescent orange and purple Naugahyde sofa in the other.

After a few pleasantries about the weather, the subtlety of Japanese tea and Flapping Heron convertible preferred shares subject to redemption, the interview began.

Q. Mr. Sashimi, your company has had record-breaking losses during the past few years. Does this mean the Japanese pickled plum industry is close to collapse or is it just a lull?
A. Yes, business has been souring a bit lately, but I predict that the next eight months will show a drastic improvement. It is written by the great Chinese philosopher Quonset Hut, in *The Book of Chang*, "Quiet perseverance yields big profit margin." After that, I'm concerned.

Q. What is your concern?
A. My concern is the total lack of restraint on the part of the American pickle exporters. My concern is the inability of the Japanese plum picklers' lobby to sway the government to make more restrictions on imports. My concern is gherkins, kosher dills, pickled tomatoes. My concern is pickled peppers and those little cocktail onions. The relish problem is also of major thrust. It is written in *The Book of Chang*, "Too many pickles in the path of the flying dragon bring burning of heart to the wanderer."

Q. So what is the real gut issue?
A. Everything boils down to the same thing: We have to decide what fair trade is all about, and we have to be competitive. Those American whippersnappers have gotten away for too long with their practice of dumping cultural impositions on us. We eat their burgers, their fried chicken, and play their baseball, but we don't make them wear kimonos or hit each other with kendo sticks, do we? It is also written in *The Book of Chang*, "The eater of pickled plums is clear-thinking and cautious, and where no one else perceives, he finds a tax shelter."

"My concern is gherkins, Kosher dills, pickled tomatoes. My concern is pickled peppers and those little cocktail onions. The relish problem is also of major thrust."

43

Q. *But it is known that the American pickles cost less than the Japanese varieties and the Japanese people love them.*
A. Yes, and it's very embarrassing. We must put our foot down. After all, it's our country and our jobs. The Japanese people must be made to understand that more American kosher dills means more social problems, more unemployment, more heartburn. As it is written in *The Book of Chang*, "You can deduct an amount each year for assets you buy to use in your business; therein lies perfection."

Q. *Don't you feel pressures to hold down costs in order to compete?*
A. I wish I were in Heinz's position, or even Vlasic's. They don't have to worry about little red pickled plums because those companies have 93 percent of the large and luxury pickle market, because, as it's written in *The Book of Chang*, "dispersion leads to a passive activity income."

Q. *Are you under pressure to expand your production into kosher varieties?*
A. Yes, but much would be involved: massive imports of dill, kosher salt, rabbis, not to even mention those funny jars with the rubber gaskets. And labor. Going into production in this area would mean hiring a huge foreign labor force. And in *The Book of Chang*, for crying out loud, it is written, "if the foreign law taxes earned income, the denominator of the fraction is the total amount of income subject to foreign tax minus deductible expenses allocable to that income."

Q *Foreign? Why couldn't you take advantage of the unemployed already in Japan and put them to useful work?*
A. Because the Americans don't know from pickled plums and the Japanese don't know from kosher dills. There is a vast sea of brine separating us, or as *The Book of Chang* reveals, "Over-consumption of salt in the diet: Arrogant dragon will have cause to repent and lose eligibility for unemployment compensation."

Q. *How about a joint venture between Japanese and American pickle producers?*
A. I could immediately predict disastrous results . . . a pickled plum the size of a basketball . . . a bright red kosher dill the size of a small marble. Corned-beef sandwiches would start tasting like rice, and sushi would be served in a sesame seed bun with a side of coleslaw. Unrest would follow and nuclear war would be just around the corner.

The interview ends as Mr. Sashimi quite abruptly rises to his full 4 feet 3 inches, introduces the interviewer to the blonde, a certain Shirley Chang, shuffles out of the room with her on his arm, and both are whisked away in a highly polished black Lincoln Continental.

SAMURAI FUNNIES

No Japanese daily newspaper is complete without a comic strip. These miniature masterpieces provide poignant insights into the trials and tribulations of the Urban Samurai's everyday life, and Samurai Funnies are no exception.

SAMURAI FUNNIES, Part One

SAMURAI FUNNIES, Part Two

O.K. Line Up and Have Fun: Culture Time in Japan

A love hotel of the Edo period

While the main cultural activities of Western man consist of watching celebrities grab their crotches, opening mail from Ed McMahon, and listening to rock music so loud it can drive nails through concrete, the Urban Samurai is recognized throughout the world for his refined cultural literacy, sophistication, and taste. His kids are taught to read at the age of three and will have breezed through entire libraries of literature while Western children are still struggling with Dick and Jane. Even as an adult, the Urban Samurai is constantly on a quest for cultural betterment, through reading, attending theatrical and musical performances, and watching television. "Aha," you say. "I do that last one a lot, and I'm accused of being a dull-witted couch potato." Esteemed reader, study the Way of the Urban Samurai and you will be able to see how even television can bring about spiritual fulfillment.

MASTERPIECES OF JAPANESE LITERATURE

Part One: Just Say Noh Drama

Noh dramas are extremely colorful, extremely complex, and extremely long. Attending one is like sitting through six Broadway plays back to back and not being able to understand any of the words. This is also why the Urban Samurai doesn't usually attend one of these cultural events until after he's dead. The following is a short synopsis of a Noh classic that would normally require the better part of a business week to perform.

"The Sumida River Twins" deals with the strife and intrigue which take place during a power struggle in a feudal California "daimyo" family. The symbolism and imagery are not only highly fantastic, they are highly unlikely. There aren't even any advertisements shown during intermission.

The feudal lord, Yoshida no Shosho Yukifusa has twin sons, Umewaka and Matsuwaka. They were given birth by his concubine, Hannyo. Actually, they were carried to full term by his wife, Kimiko, but the due date conflicted with her bowling night. Hannyo's father, Hitachi Taijo Momotsura, is a money grubbing sneak and schemes to take over the hamburger fortune of the Yoshida family and diversify into tomato by-products. He is so greedy that he would only allow Hannyo to marry on the condition that Yukifusa take over the payments on his Mercedes and throw in a starter set of crystal as well.

He convinces Yukifusa that a certain giant cedar is spoiling the view and must be cut down, when in fact the tree is endowed with supernatural powers. Yukifusa makes the second biggest mistake of his life (the first being his marriage to Hannyo) and cuts down the tree. Cursed by the spirit of the cedar, he becomes a concert pianist. He performs in all the major cities

Umewaka heads for the Bay area

49

of the world to packed houses, but fails to win the admiration of the press because his kimono sleeves keep getting caught between the keys, especially during the f minor Mazurka op. 50, no. 1 of Chopin. With regret he retires, takes up singing advertising jingles through comb and tissue paper, and is shortly thereafter committed to a mental institution.

To make matters worse, Matsuwaka is abducted by a long-nosed "tengu" goblin, which is the way recruiters for aluminum siding companies looked in those days. Having been promised lifetime employment and a subscription to "Aluminum Siding Highlights" he settles into his work making telephone sales. In the meantime, the other twin son, Umewaka, who has been dabbling lately in visuals and recently coated the entire city of La Jolla with a layer of Glidden pink spread satin exterior acrylic, paints an eye on the carp drawn on an invaluable scroll entrusted to the Yoshida family by the emperor. The carp, thus given life, leaps out of the scroll, disguises itself as a presidential candidate and gets involved in a slimy sex scandal. When his true identity is revealed, a poll is taken and he is broiled in lemon butter and consumed by several members of a small church in Menasha, Wisconsin.

The insurance company refuses to make a settlement for damages done to the scroll, Hannyo's hair begins to fall out by the handful, and Umewaka runs away from home leaving everything behind but his IBM compatible lap top. Driven by wanderlust he heads for the San Francisco Bay area and finds employment with a skin flick producer, Sarushima Sota, who is actually a former Yoshida family retainer named Awaji Shichiro, although by this time no one can remember the names, anyway. Learning the identity of Umewaka, Shichiro vows to repent, become a public restroom attendant and work for the cause of his former master's family. He then downs a complete steak dinner, three milkshakes, and half a dozen twinkies, shoots up with Novocain and commits *hara-kiri*.

Hannyo, who has gone crazy from grief over the loss of her hair and the loss of a story line, is led by the spirit of Shichiro and moves to an Eastern suburb of Cleveland. While under the hairdryer, she prays for the reputation of her ill-fated son. During the comb-out, a "tengu", the incarnation of Shichiro's spirit comes, bringing Matsuwaka, who is wearing a Sister Souljah tee shirt and high top sneakers, a large meatloaf and an entire set of Tupper-ware with him. Handing Matsuwaka over to Hannyo, the "tengu" disappears into thin air, whistling a Scarlatti sonata. The House of Yoshida is rehabilitated, relocates to Phoenix and opens a successful chain of gourmet bagel bars throughout the Southwest.

MASTERPIECES OF JAPANESE LITERATURE

Part Two: Haiku

Haiku is that sparse type of poetry with images that seem always to hover on the periphery of reality, but get closer to the truth than that cumbersome prose style found in Western literature. The three-line verse form (of, respectively, five, seven, and five syllables) is often shorter than the title of a corresponding Western work of similar importance.

Thus, *The Literature, Notation and Performance of Left-handed Plucked-String Instruments from the Medieval to the Early Baroque in Eastern European Civilization* can have the essence of its entire 925 pages (plus 30 pages of footnotes) described in 17 succinct syllables:

> Countless silken strings,
> Frenzied fingers pluck wildly:
> Crazy lute player.

The following examples of haiku describe the fragile but exquisite beauty of contemporary Japanese life:

> Home at two a.m.,
> Sushi, beer, and sake breath:
> Large expense account.

> Beef too expensive,
> Hold the ketchup and pickles:
> Rice and fish again.

> Yellow rubber gloves,
> Undulating vacuum hose:
> Night-dirt collectors.

> Fast food and light beer,
> Instant gratification,
> Ozone depletion.

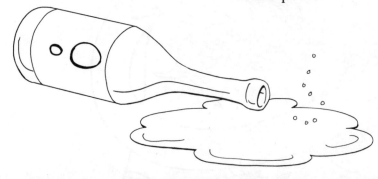

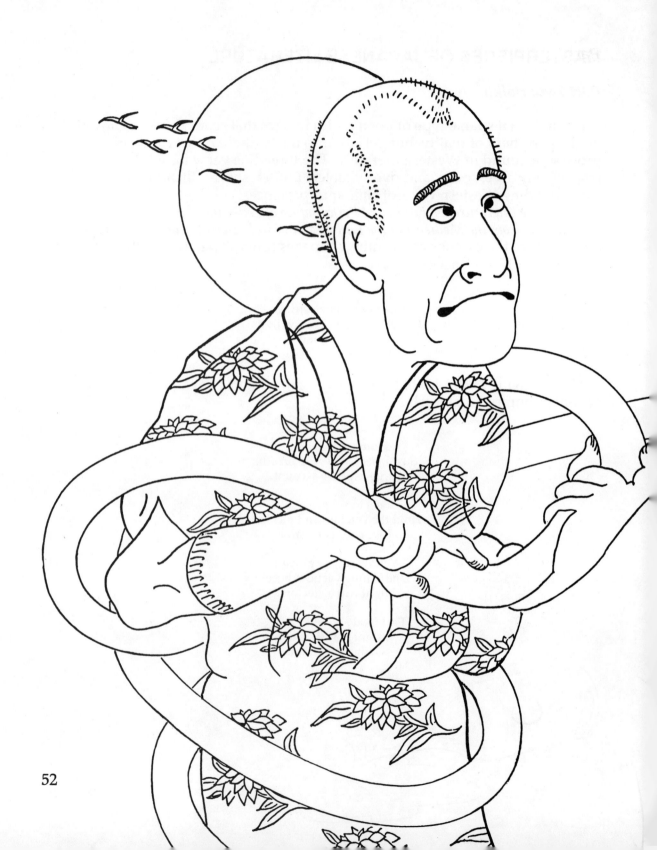

Part Three: Lowku

The Four Seasons:

Summer

An outdoor steambath
The brain deep-fried in the sun
Japanese summer

Fall

Rainrainrainrainrain
An occasional typhoon
rainrainrainrainrain

Winter

No insulation
A frozen posterior
Winter in Tokyo

Spring

Porno, love hotels
Pink cherry blossoms explode
A young man's fancy.

RELAXING AT HOME

The Urban Samurai Sensory Deprivation Tank

A temple of serenity, the interior of the Urban Samurai's house is so cleverly designed that he can wander into his neighbor's home by mistake and not know the difference for two weeks, at which time he realizes his underwear chafes and his brand of toothpaste has been switched. By the crass Western way of thinking, his house is downright drafty. But to him, his tiny but airy dwelling is built so that he may enjoy himself in a refreshing and inspirational setting as close to nature as possible, even though his monthly rent is slightly more than that of the entire World Trade Center. Heaters and air-conditioners are never used but are there only as a reminder to the weak that one must suffer for an ideal. In the preparation for even more severe hardships in the battle of life (getting up on Monday morning, a weekend with the in-laws, running out of coffee, for example), the Urban Samurai is grateful for, indeed welcomes such psyche-strengtheners.

The walls are an earthen-clay compound punctuated by handsome wooden beams. The floors are tightly woven tatami mats. Sliding door and window coverings are snow-white paper behind simple wooden lattices. The two main furnishings are a low table at which the Urban Samurai seats himself cross-legged and a large high definition color television equipped with a VCR. Artfully crammed into this compact room, in which the farthest wall is always an arm's length away, are a doily-draped davenport and an overstuffed chair purchased when "Leave It to Beaver" was first televised. Their function is to hold items which have overflowed from the various shelves, sideboards, and glass knickknack boxes also in the room, which has been accented with a small vacuum cleaner, magazines, and periodicals so old that they are glued shut. Several weeks worth of laundry hanging inside because of the rain complete the decor.

It is into this world of exquisite beauty that the Urban Samurai will enter. Silently as a Noh player, he sheds his everyday worries, his weapons and woes, and glides into a refuge of harmony and grace. He takes his place and sits motionless — Zen-like — sometimes for days. Even the babble of the television, placed a reverential two feet away from the Urban Samurai's face, becomes a mantra through which he transcends to the bliss of nirvana. (Zen monks do this, too, but with the sound turned down.) It helps him become one with nature. It also helps drown out the screaming wife and kids; the motorcycles, cars, and trucks revving and thundering past his house; loudspeakers blasting; jackhammers pounding; electric guitars reverberating — all only a paper wall away.

The ultimate aim of Zen is, by means of meditation, to rid one's mind of all the concepts and emotions that encumber it. This is why television is so important in Japan.

URBAN SAMURAI TV HIGHLIGHTS

3:00-4:30
"Mrs. Satoko Saccaroid's Cooking School": Taken up in today's program are the problems of the 37-degree angle cut. Seventh in a 15 week series on cucumber cutting. Today's guests, popular singers Keiko Crablegs and Terri Yakki will describe, by means of intricate facial expressions and tight camera close-ups, the actual taste of a cucumber cut on a 37-degree angle. A special feature on today's program will be filmed highlights of Greta Geisha's recent "All-Japan Cucumber Caravan," during which she sampled cucumbers cut according to each area's unique traditions.

4:30-5:00
"Let's Weather": Today's forecast will be preempted by a special live broadcast of this week's parliamentary debate on the fate of the 3.1 billion umbrellas held in Japan Railway's lost and found.

5:01-6:01
"Urban Samurai Evangelical Hour": Brother Suzuki, president of Mitsutomo Heavy Industries, will lead an hour of prayer and stock reports. Featured on today's show will be true-to-life testimonials by three devoted members of the Mitsutomo flock, broadcast live from the floor of the Yokohama plant, where hush money for sexual favors paid in one month represents more than half of the G.N.P of the entire free world.

5:00-5:01
"My Goodness!": This moving drama is about the tragedy of a housewife whose husband, dissatisfied with his work, decides to stay home all day. In this evening's episode, while looking through the refrigerator for a snack, the husband stumbles upon ruins of a pre-Incan civilization the wife had carefully hidden behind the mayonnaise.

6:02-6:17
"My Cute World of Furry and Feathered Friends": The interesting ecology and habits of the stuffed derma, a small gallinaceous bird that usually inhabits the cracks of all-concrete housing developments and feeds on heavy metals, will be introduced in today's animal documentary-quiz show, hosted by popular singers Keiko Crablegs and Terri Yakki.

6:17-6:19
"Ah, My Persimmon, Part 38": Drama about an apple-cheeked, pigtailed country girl who enrolls in a tough Tokyo high school. Madcap trouble bestirs when it is revealed that she is actually a 35-year-old male unemployed triple agent for the KGB.

6:19-6:25
"Housewives' World of Economics": Today's distinguished panel, hosted by popular singers Keiko Crablegs and Terri Yakki, discusses the far-reaching implications of the devaluation of the *baht* and what it means to your divorce settlement. On the book review section of the program will be a 20-second in-depth look at L. Ron Takahashi's latest blockbuster, *Megazen*. This slim unpretentious volume on Japanese business management techniques is the book that has taken the Western world by storm, causing everyone who reads it to trade in their BMWs for Honda Civics, file for bankruptcy, and shave their heads.

6:25-7:17
"Let's English": Spotlighted in today's language lesson is the word *cat*. Also featured on this broadcast is special guest Mr. Morris V. Bialosky, a taxi driver of the Bronx, U.S.A., who will lecture on nonverbal communication. He will demonstrate several hand and finger gestures indigenous to species of his native land.

7:17-9:00
"My Cute Quiz": Quiz show. In this daredevil contest of nerves, two teams of popular singers, headed by popular singers Keiko Crablegs and Terri Yakki, try to guess the difference between a stuffed koala bear and the *I Ching*.

9:00-10:30
"Let's Fun": Children's contest. Grade school and junior high school students challenge each other in setting up a domino chain that requires not only intensive physical patience, but spiritual concentration as well: if dropped, each domino would release on impact enough deadly methyl-di-zircocyanide to wipe the entire population of Tokyo off the map.

10:30-11:00
"Famous Japanese Disasters": A former high-ranking department store chain executive, now serving his 12th year of incarceration, reveals his agony and shame when it was discovered that a staff member had been gift-wrapping packages from right to left, instead of from left to right.

11:00-1:12 A.M.
"Fade-Out": Talk-show hosts Keiko Crablegs and Terri Yakki attempt to talk.

59

SAMURAI FUNNIES, Part Three

TRAVEL

An Urban Samurai in Paris

Because of the ever-soaring value of the yen and some really clever business practices on the part of the Japan Travel Bureau, it costs more for the Urban Samurai to visit his great uncle in North Tuna Prefecture, Japan, than it does to take a trip abroad. The resulting sightseeing boom is attracting tens of thousands of Japanese, usually all traveling together at the same time. Everywhere in the world there is a tourist attraction, be it Niagara Falls, the Grand Canyon, or the Dr. Scholl Footcare Factory, that ubiquitous group, herded along by a conservatively dressed young Japanese woman wearing white gloves and carrying a little banner, can be seen. Recently a large group of Japanese tourists was observed floating down the Atlantic seaboard on *Mobro*, the refuse barge, busily snapping pictures and pocketing souvenir garbage fragments encased in Lucite.

The only major drawback, other than the difficulty in accommodating half the population of Osaka at the Super Eight Motel in Sioux Falls, is the inability of the host country to provide the Urban Samurai with his own food. While a Westerner can thrive, an Urban Samurai cannot subsist, even for an hour or two, on a diet of Doritos, Coke, and pizza, even a pizza with anchovies. If the Urban Samurai should walk into an Italian restaurant he will order spaghetti with soy sauce and forest mushrooms. Substitute a cup of Nestea Instant for his coveted green tea and he will react as if Mount Fuji had been leveled and turned into a parking garage.

How does the Urban Samurai, then, deal with the culinary trauma of being outside of his own native land? Simple. He will bring his own food. He will take a once-in-a-lifetime three-day and two-night sightseeing tour to Paris, and you will find him in his room at the Ritz, surreptitiously slurping one of 40 or so bowls of instant noodles he has brought with him.

And why noodles? Rice may be the lifeblood of the Urban Samurai, but noodles are his emotional release. The consumption of one bowl of noodles is the Japanese equivalent of six months of therapy. Thanks to a unique facial muscle lacking in all other races and nationalities, the Urban Samurai is able to literally vacuum the correct number of noodles, along with the required amount of boiling hot broth, into his mouth with more velocity than is required for tests in the wind tunnel of the NASA Jet Propulsion Laboratory. This procedure not only helps him cope with the difficulties of everyday life, but it brings him closer to nirvana than meditation at the Zen rock garden at Ryoanji temple.

THE URBAN SAMURAI
CRASH COURSE

THE URBAN SAMURAI CRASH COURSE, PART ONE

The One-Minute Samurai

For those of you who feel that it is just not enough to understand the Urban Samurai, but must actually become one, I have included The Urban Samurai Crash Course, a condensed version of the renowned seventeenth-century treatise by Miyamoto Musashi. By following this course, you'll see how simple and easy a cosmic merging as one with the universe can be.

Here is a series of exercises, taking only a minute each, that will improve your progress towards samuraization:

1. Your wife serves lasagna with the most gorgeous cheese filling ever beheld by mankind. You are totally famished and truly believe you could polish off the entire casserole single-handedly. You tighten your belt, count silently to ten, pick up and glance through the paper, and leave the room.

2. Your girlfriend enters the room wearing nothing but pasties and a g-string. You can barely withstand the arousal and want to throw her onto the sofa. Instead, you lean over, switch channels, and proceed to watch with intense concentration "The World of Fishing" on PBS.

3. You resist jumping out of your chair to switch the channel, even though you realize you are about to view an episode of "Little House on the Prairie" you have seen 14 other times.

4. You are alone on an otherwise deserted beach. The most beautiful woman you have ever seen in your entire life comes and arranges her towel 5 inches away from yours, unhooks her bikini top and proceeds to sun herself. You do nothing and proceed to memorize your computer printout detailing 30 years of Albanian economic trends.

THE URBAN SAMURAI CRASH COURSE, PART TWO

Enlightenment is just around the corner, but how about beefing up that vocabulary a little with:

A Glossary of Urban Samurai Terms

Extramarital sex: The only way to get any.

Food processor: Wife, girlfriend, mother, or any female over the age of 12.

Foreplay: A golf term.

Futon: A tropical storm.

High impact aerobics: How extracting one's self from the rush hour train is achieved.

Hostile takeover: Coming home from work and discovering that the locks have been changed.

Premature ejaculation: What happens to the cassette when you press the wrong button on the VCR.

Sexual aids: Toupee and porno video.

Soy sauce: *vt* to get drunk (slang).

Stress: What is put upon the tatami floor when the new color television is delivered.

Sushi: A small asexual spore occuring in a certain fungus.

Tatami: A native Mexican delicacy consisting of minced meat and red peppers, rolled in corn meal, wrapped in corn husks, and sent to Japan for flooring materials.

Tofu: A hard, chewy candy.

THE URBAN SAMURAI CRASH COURSE, PART THREE

Whoever said that Westerners have a lower IQ than Japanese was greatly mistaken; you're doing so well that you are now ready for:

The Urban Samurai Quiz

1. Do you have the ability to remain expressionless when told your fly is open?

2. Are you repulsed when your wife accidentally brushes against you when she's walking by?

3. Can you remain motionless in front of the television even after the same twenty second commercial for a feminine hygiene product has been broadcast 40 times in one hour?

4. Do you believe enlightenment can be attained by nonverbal means, such as racing in front of all the other cars in order to be the first one at the red light?

5. Do you believe the serving of leftovers is a crime against humanity?

6. Do you think your mother would have been a better match for the emperor than empress Michiko?

7. Even if your all-time favorite strawberry shortcake with real whipped cream is being served, do you not only resist jumping up and down and clapping your hands, but also refrain from cracking a smile?

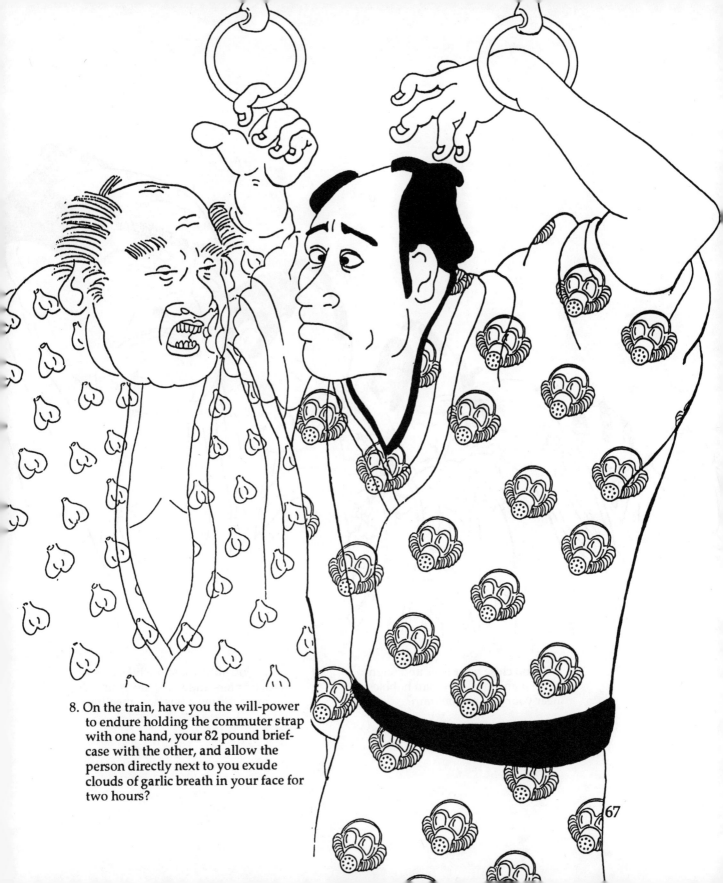

8. On the train, have you the will-power
   to endure holding the commuter strap
   with one hand, your 82 pound briefcase with the other, and allow the
   person directly next to you exude
   clouds of garlic breath in your face for
   two hours?

67

9. Will you close your eyes and feign
   sleep if an elderly woman hobbles
   near your seat on the train?

10. Can you sit stock still while a cock-
    roach enters and walks up your
    pantleg during a business meeting?

68

SCORING

The abysmally low score of one to three "yeses" indicates not only your love of quiche and ballet, but that you actually live with your mother-in-law. You are a hopeless wuss. (Recommended remedial reading: *Eating with chopsticks*, volume 1.)

It is obvious from your score of four to six "yeses" that you not only help set the table, you dry the dishes as well. You are rather far from the goal.

A score of seven to nine "yeses" shows that you are definitely the strong, silent type and qualify for samuraiship. You must, however, refrain from complimenting your wife or girlfriend on her cooking.

If you answered every question with "yes," within your stainless steel cranium is a boulder of solid granite. You already are an Urban Samurai.

SAMURAI FUNNIES, Part Four

The Urban Samurai
Workout Book

Japan is definitely not the country in which to participate in field sports unless, of course, the designated field is no larger than a 3-by-5 file card. Because of this, the Urban Samurai has dedicated himself throughout the centuries to such sports as kendo, judo, and locating his bicycle at the station, activities that are perfectly suited to his acute ability for concentration and do not take up the room football, bungee-cord jumping, or following your dog around with a pooper-scooper require.

In recent years, however, space has become so limited that even the traditional martial arts are being crowded out. Since needlepoint and national telethons don't seem likely alternatives, how does the Urban Samurai stay in shape? Jogging in place is not the answer because of the pounding strain it puts on the tatami-mat floors; likewise flailing the limbs about aerobic style would do severe damage to the sliding paper walls, as well as to the other occupants of the room. Sprinting to and from the commuter train is also not satisfactory because it does not fulfill the Urban Samurai's emotional needs.

After ten years of rigorous testing and research, *The Official Urban Samurai Workout Book* has been compiled by consensus at the Japanese National Institute for Aesthetic Muscular Development, and its program is now being followed by 89% of the male population of Japan. Following are excerpts from the book.

HOW TO KEEP FIT IN JAPAN
BY MEANS OTHER THAN RUNNING IN PLACE

The Urban Samurai does not need extravagant equipment or space-age technology to keep his body taut and trim. In simply the time it takes to get from home to work — on the average, a bracing two- to three-hour commute — you can maintain your lean waistline by converting two conventional umbrellas into a multi-use, variable-resistance rowing machine. Used during the height of rush hour, it will provide maximum resistance; and today's on-the-go Urban Samurai knows that a muscle needs constant challenge to remain vigorous.

The basic workout begins by looking for a seat on the train, usually accomplished after an hour or so of pushing and shoving. Once seated, hold the umbrella handles near your torso, with the tips firmly planted on the floor of the train.

Sitting on the comfortable padded seat, slowly push the handles away from you, breathing deeply and feeling the springlike resistance caused by the passengers crammed in directly in front of you. Letting your hip flexors do most of the work, but without lessening the tension in your body, slowly describe a wide arc with each arm, and finally, pushing your fellow commuters away, bring the umbrella handles back to their original positions.

For the Urban Samurai who is unable to get a seat on the train, the following two exercises are made to order. Slip your feet into two adjacent commuter straps and clasp your hands behind your head. Bending at the waist, slowly bring your body parallel to the floor and make gravity work for you. This simple exercise will relieve back pain and aching muscles as well as improve circulation and energy levels.

Designed with the commuter in mind, the effectiveness of this exercise increases proportionately with the number of passengers surrounding you.

NERVOUSNESS AS A FORM OF AEROBIC CONDITIONING

Here's another exercise that is inconspicuous and can be done according to the highest principles of harmony and cooperation with your fellow commuter. Upon regaining your consciousness after the train lurches forward and 400 men suddenly press against you in a communal Heimlich maneuver, bring one arm out — the one not holding the briefcase — and with the palm turned outward, grab the commuter strap nearest you. It will be in use by five or six others, so your exercise is ready to begin. Move the strap toward you by bending your body at the waist, keeping knees in a locked position. Feel the mounting physical pressure as the train grinds to a halt for each station. Your torso will feel like an aluminum beer can in a garbage compactor when commuters squeeze past you to leave. Counteract this by panicking as you think of your briefcase which has relocated itself to the other side of the train. Now eliminate all thoughts except for that feeling of release and invigoration when, at your stop, you are propelled out of the train and you can light up.

REMOTE-CONTROL FINGER PUMPING

Turn those flabby fingers into precision instruments with remote control finger pumping. To get the most benefit from this workout, each finger must be pushed to full capacity through its entire range of movement. Although this exercise varies with cable subscribers, the accompanying illustration demonstrates how each finger muscle is fully challenged at every point of its contraction, even during reruns. Please also refer to the chapter on high impact chopstick usage.

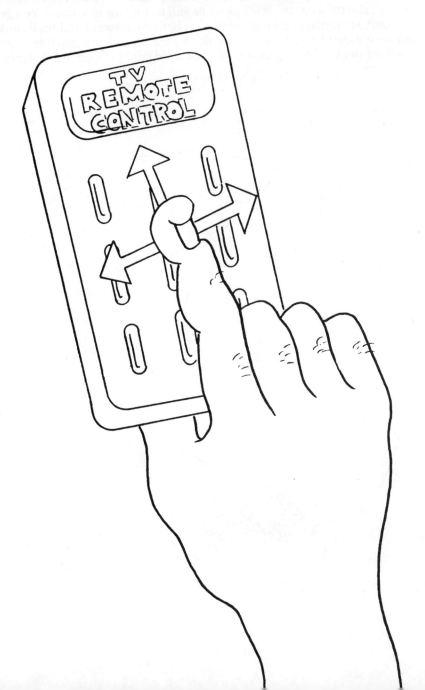

THE WARM-DOWN

The next illustration demonstrates the ease with which the busy executive Urban Samurai can develop and tone his forearms as well as trim thighs and hips and firm arms and chest. Sitting as pictured, thumb and fingers firmly gripping on a twelve ounce glass, television screen squarely in view, you begin your workout by pushing the left arm forward and down as far as possible without spilling the beer. As your abdominals contract you feel an invigorating warmth. Pause for a moment and slowly raise the glass to your lips while still feeling the resistance. You get twice the workout, strengthening your muscles on both the forward and back strokes, and improving circulation and coordination by the precise and exacting movement involved in placing the glass on the table after your fifteenth refill. Repeat with the right arm.

The Urban Samurai
Kissing Manual

ORAL SEX, PART ONE

What to Do Before Smoking

Unless there is a major sports tournament about to go into its final climax, complete loss of hair within a 24 hour period, or the disappearance of the television set, eating is clearly the focal point of the Urban Samurai's existence. Thus, the conclusions reached by the Japanese Institute for Social Research, located on the second floor of East Radish's Golden Condom Love Capsule Hotel, do not come as a surprise.

According to the data, the Urban Samurai does not like to kiss. (That fondling motion he does with his lips around the filter end of the cigarette does not count). The formation of his kisses are in correlation not with the lady in question, but with what tasty morsel would titillate his taste buds at that particular moment.

Therefore, the most efficient method by which to sexually arouse an Urban Samurai is to whisper sweet murmurings such as "broiled eel" or "fermented soybeans" into his ear. The following chart depicts the eight major kissing configurations employed by the Urban Samurai and the food which inspires each one.

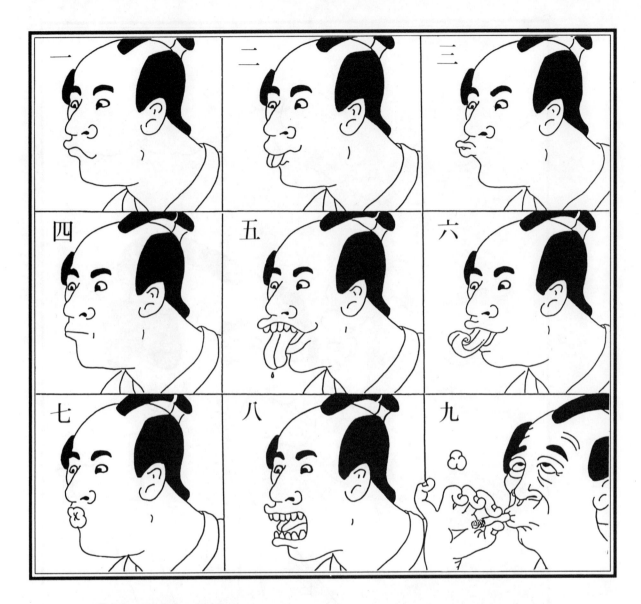

一 Chicken omelet over rice
二 Chinese noodle soup
三 Octopus
四 Take-out burger
五 Sushi
六 Sea urchin
七 Pickled plum
八 Kobe beef steak
九 See next page

That fondling motion he does with his lips around the
filter end of the cigarette does not count.

"Pass the soy sauce, I'm coming!"

Wife of the Urban Samurai

Because the Urban Samurai spends almost all of his waking hours either at the office, commuting, drinking with the boys, or watching the tube, he is not able to develop the delicate skills Westerners tend to take for granted in marital interaction, like picking his teeth at the table or recognizing his wife. Therefore, the wife carries the responsibility of spousal solicitude. Before a marriage can take place, a standardized test, developed by the Ministry of Health and Welfare, is given to the bride-to-be to make sure her abilities are up to par. If she fails the test more than twice, she is exiled to Detroit, enrolled in a video dating service, and forced to go out for coffee dates three times a day for ten years.

WIFE OF SAMURAI QUIZ

Do you read *The Journal of the Philosophy of Social Structures and Economic Dynamics* or do simple things like explaining the structure of the universe elude you? Is your mind just a void waiting to be filled with enlightenment by an Urban Samurai? Find out if you are a match for the Urban Samurai by answering the following questions:

1. Is the 50th anniversary of the invention of Teflon the most important date on your calendar?

2. Are you able to perceive beauty and truth in dirty laundry?

3. Do you think of your man in affectionate terms like Attila the Hun?

4. Do you think a floppy disk is a cucumber sliced too thin?

5. Can you express profound sympathy when your husband gives a detailed description of his hemorrhoid at the dinner table for the 14th day in a row.

6. Is the highlight of your day watching "Captain Koala Bear" on TV, even when your kids are already in high school?

7. Do you have to ask for permission from your mother-in-law to go out, go to the lavatory, or go into labor?

8. Are you able to achieve tranquillity by doing the dishes with a 25 pound baby strapped to your back?

9. Would you qualify for a black belt in silent suffering if there were such a thing?

10. Do you think a dividend reinvestment plan is serving leftovers?

SCORING

Ten "yeses" show that you are able to attain an aura of complete vacuity on a moment's notice. You are already the wife of an Urban Samurai and are on the path to illumination.

Seven to ten "yeses" indicate a sufficiently servile personality. You would be a fine match for an Urban Samurai if only you would cover your mouth when you smile.

From a dismal score of four to six "yeses," it is apparent that you read the Wall Street Journal and have the old man washing dishes. The Urban Samurai may not be for you.

One to three "yeses." Not only does this catastrophic score show that you refuse to live with your mother-in-law and have the kids at day-care, but that you actually can change a tire.

"SAYONARA, DEAR"

A Dinner Time Story

As we discussed in the chapter on communication, verbal economy is one of the most distinctive features of the Urban Samurai. Since to him effusion reveals a shallow understanding of the conditions of the universe, the Urban Samurai is not famous for his dinnertime discourse. Due to the fact that during this time his entire being is fixated on the television screen (a kind of divine contemplation), it is up to the lady of the house to hold up both ends of the conversation.

Wife: Dear, you'll really like this bamboo-shoot dish. My aunt from Noodle Heights called today. Well, why don't you at least try this broiled fish? She said their house burned down last night and they'd have to build a new one. The steamed spinach is just the way you like it, sprinkled with dried fish flakes and soy sauce. Just like mother used to make, huh? I said the six of them could move into our apartment while the house is under construction — seven months or so. Their kids are really cute. Can you imagine, four kids in five years, and that two-year-old is such a scream. I guess you'll have to put your antique blown-glass collection away for a while. The chicken in cream sauce is delicious. I wish you'd try it. You know I bust my buns cooking for you and you don't even look at it. I told them you'd be able to come up with $300,000 or so to help get them on their feet again. It's the least you can do. Those fish eggs were pretty expensive, you know. I don't even bother getting the cheaper ones since you made such a scene last time. Here's the tofu and fish-paste stew you didn't eat last night. I freshened it up with a few snow peas. If we don't eat it tonight I'll have to give it to the neighbor's dog. Do you want your rice and soup now? I made some of your favorite Chinese cabbage pickles, too. They'll be moving in tomorrow. Uncle wears the same size you do so that'll work out fine. After I get them settled, I'll leave you the phone number where I can be reached in Afghanistan.

Husband: Hey, get up and switch to channel 12 and while you're up bring me a beer.

A GLOSSARY OF TERMS FOR
THE WIFE OF THE URBAN SAMURAI

Body substance isolation procedures: Getting the kids to wash before dinner.

Body fakes: Pretending you like it.

Commodity speculation: Wondering if he'll eat what you made for dinner.

Home improvement: Having hubby get transferred to another city — alone.

Hyper space: A new work area you discover by balancing your cutting board on top of the dirty dishes in the sink.

Interface: That stuff they put in collars to prevent them from drooping.

Mismatched communication protocol: When he says he was with the boys and you say he wasn't.

Preferred bond: Marriage into a "better" family.

Vibrator: A seat at the end of the express train.

Women's lib: Filing for divorce.

THE URBAN SAMURAI'S GROUNDS FOR DIVORCE

1. Serving food out of Tupperware containers.

2. Touching him in public.

3. Touching him in private.

4. Telling him how you like it.

5. Accidentally erasing last night's wrestling match between Killer Kahn and Animal Hamaguchi.

6. Reading the paper over his shoulder.

7. Getting the angle wrong on the cucumber.

8. Placing the teacup on the table too loudly.

9. Asking him to pass the soy sauce.

10. Asking him to discuss it.

Grounds for divorce

92

What's wrong with this picture?

The J-Spot

THE URBAN SAMURAI PSYCHE
AND THE ORIGIN OF QUALITY CONTROL

Economists around the world were recently startled to learn the true origins of quality control, the pursuit of zero defects. A team of ethno-biologists at the International Center for Scientific Research in Prosaic, New Jersey, have finally found the explanation for what sets the Urban Samurai apart from the rest of humanity. The unique Japanese eye for detail, beauty, and precision at long last has scientific grounds.

Using the imaging technique, Positron Emission Tomography, or PET, the reseachers have discovered a cluster of neurons found only in the Japanese male brain. Referred to as the J-spot, this extraordinary part of the Japanese neural anatomy controls a special kind of awareness characterized by an ability to respond to ideas, images, and feelings so infinitesimal in detail that Westen man could not comprehend them even if they were presented to him in the centerfold of the leading porn magazine.

The J-spot allows the Urban Samurai to do whatever he does better, with more intensity, and with deeper conviction than any other member of the human race.

THE URBAN SAMURAI AUDIOPHILE

Aural Sex, Part One

For example, take a typical American stereo buff. He will simply flick on his set, sit back, and enjoy. A Samurai audio aficionado has a bigger, more complex involvement. His amplifier, pre-amplifier, balanced interconnects, transimpedence modules, bi-polar radiators, as well as his FM broadcast monitor connected to an aerial that moves in millimicrons in accordance with the rotation of the earth, will be built into the family Buddhist altar. His conviction is so deep that he would just as soon become a phonograph record so that he may be subtly fused together into a single flowing existence with his turntable. Other times he may know true serenity in reincarnation as a compact disc, and be able to reach heights of pure ecstasy being thrust into a CD transport and digital decoding computer.

His speakers, which take up two-thirds of the entire house, will be moved to their proper positions in increments indiscernible to the naked eye. All possible speaker positions will be cataloged and annotated in chronological order in an embossed leather-bound record book which is willed to his first-born son. He will fiddle with and adjust his system with manic precision, and it will be done to the exclusion of everything except smoking.

A small shelf to hold his glossy high-end audio trade magazines — at least four subscriptions of which he possesses the last 15 year's publications — will be erected in the lavatory. He will develop a tofulike complexion from lack of sun and will become headachey and irritable from loss of sleep and nourishment.

PICKINESS AS CENTER OF THE COLLECTIVE UNCONSCIOUS

Why Freud Would Have Had a Field Day in Japan

The J-spot thus manifests itself in a preoccupation with fastidiousness and extends to all components of Japanese life. Each individal fruit is coddled by farmers with the utmost care to prevent blemishes, bruises, and wormholes (which is why one melon may cost more than a week's vacation in the Caribbean). Packages are so beautifully wrapped that the contents are usually a let-down. Dustcovers are protected by dustcovers, and the dust itself is carefully collected and airmailed to the poor investment brokers in Europe.

The most apparent indication of fussiness is seen in clothing. The Urban Samurai himself is, of course, alway correctly and tastefully attired, shoes shined, hair neatly trimmed, the company pin in place on his impeccably designed lapel. Neckties are chosen each morning by statistical analysis. Lift the newspapers off a bum (referred to in Japan as a "pre-social technician") sleeping on a park bench or in the railroad station, and you will find him dressed with more taste and care than the average American young urban professional. Even the pre-social technician's matching paper bags are marked "Gucci." On his days off, he works in a major company as a personal image consultant.

Other members of Japanese society as well would not be caught dead without the requisite apparel and accessories. Trash collectors are outfitted by Brooks Brothers and stuffed animals come complete with three-piece navy blue suits, attaché cases and authenticated family lineage registrations. Not surprisingly, scientists have observed that the Japanese strain of *E. coli* bacteria is much more refined and elegant than its Western counterpart.

Thanks to the J-spot, a Japanese male can calibrate
the rotation of an electron on a star 8 zillion light
years away, but can't tell when his wife has PMS.

EATING HABITS (ORAL SEX, PART TWO)

While Western man requires intensive training in order to detect and describe a variety of tastes and smell, he is usually unable to progress beyond three or four varieties, including hot and cold. The Urban Samurai, on the other hand, is naturally endowed with sensory capabilities which give him the ability to pass judgement on over 80,000 components of taste and smell. The accompanying chart depicts the intricate system of taste regions of the Urban Samurai as compared with the areas of primitive taste perception of Western man. The following charts illustrate the intricate functions of the Urban Samurai's olfactory senses as opposed to those of Western man.

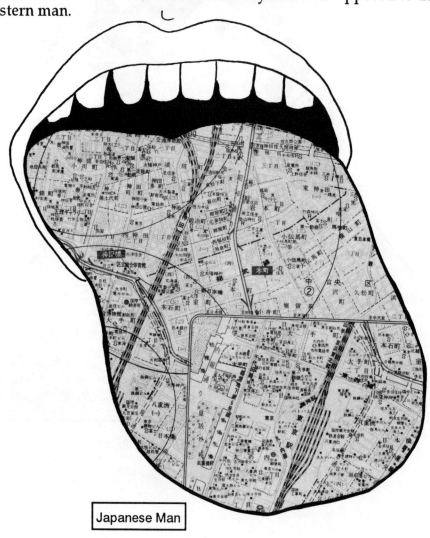

Japanese Man

100

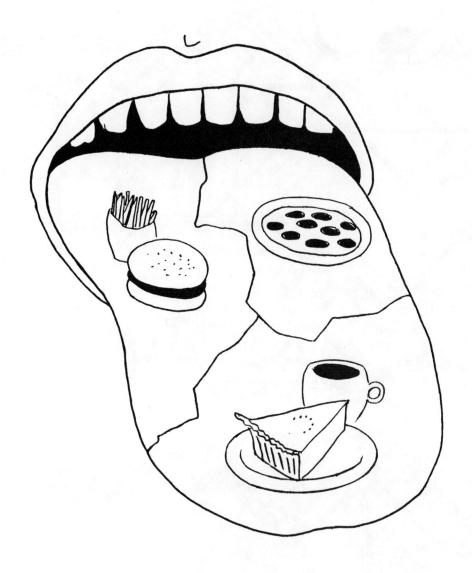

Western Man

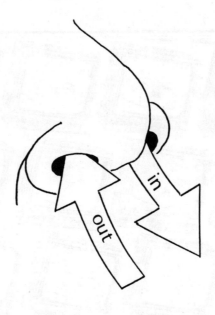

Western Man

Son of the Urban Samurai

APTITUDE TEST FOR MOTHERS-OF-FUTURE-URBAN SAMURAI

The most important key to the inner workings of the Urban Samurai is held by his mother. Your husband may be over the hill, but it is not too late to train your son to be an authentic Urban Samurai. The main job of a Japanese mother is to keep one step ahead in her children's studies so she can coach them at home. Because a typical male child spends an average of four hours a day watching television and the rest of his time playing video games, it is extremely important for his mother to make efficient use of those precious seconds he spends changing channels.

The following test was compiled by child-psychologist/anthropologist, Nesselrode Pin, who urges preparation from the eighth month before birth.

The correct answers are discussed in Dr. Pin's forthcoming book, *An Etiological Analysis of Japanese School Uniforms: The Uses of Navy Blue in Childhood*, coauthored by Dennis Overbite and Extrabooks N. Pigpen. The reference section of the book offers an excellent evaluation of high-level mathematics, linguistic and social studies preparatory schools for toddlers, as well as a detailed breakdown of entrance requirements and ways to skirt them.

1. Your mother-in-law has announced in your fourth month of pregnancy that you are carrying a girl, and she wants a grandson. You:
    a. order out for Thai food with four red peppers
    b. join a traveling rock band.
    c. change doctors.
    d. eat 17 pickled plums in a row every morning for two months and receive acupuncture in your shins.

2. The baby arrives and — Buddha is merciful — it is a boy. You:
    a. order a miniature three-piece business suit with matching navy blue gabardine diapers from the department store.
    b. thank your mother-in-law.
    c. begin arranging his marriage.
    d. make an application to The Tokyo University School of Law.

3. The baby reaches the 33rd day of his life. You:
    a. would like to inform your husband, but are afraid to wake him up.
    b. would like to inform your husband, but aren't sure whether that is he or the life-insurance salesman at the door.
    c. check your research on the pineal cells in cross-sections of hamster brains.
    d. pick your husband up at the pachinko parlor on the way to the Shinto shrine for the naming ceremony.

4. The baby is now crawling and cannot be let out of your sight for a minute. You:
   a. strap him to your back for the next three years.
   b. quit your job at the factory in order to accompany him to his violin lessons.
   c. have an affair with the rice delivery boy.
   d. trade him in for a 12-piece designer set of black lace peek-a-boo underwear.

5. Your baby, now a two-year-old toddler, is beginning to cause an undue amount of mischief. You try to distract him by:
   a. letting him take apart the engine in your husband's Porsche.
   b. balancing a column of twenty eight bowls of instant noodles on your chin every day for an hour.
   c. swinging from the light fixture while holding a dripping newspaper full of garbage.
   d. introducing him to your husband.

6. Your three year old is showing signs of readiness to enter nursery school. You:
   a. enroll him in a quantum mechanics cram course.
   b. allow him to eat only if he can conjugate the verb *to compel* in Serbo-Croatian.
   c. wear a black armband for a month if he cries.
   d. make an appointment for yourself for open-heart surgery.

7. Your back is starting to hurt from carrying him around so much. You:
   a. cut down on your intake of heavy metals.
   b. sign up for the local ladies' mud-wrestling team.
   c. rocket your arms over your head and shout "banzai" three times each time he wants to be picked up.
   d. shave your head and become a Buddhist nun.

JAPAN'S REBELLIOUS YOUTH

Today's Punks, Tomorrow's Landlords

Erosion of old family values, stress at school, and a feeling of persecution caused by the purposelessness of endless blocks of tofu and balls of rice all incite rebellion among the youth of Japan. It comes as no surprise that in a society where a couple of kindergarten exams can determine one's future in Japan's highly competitive economy, teenagers are venting their frustrations in anti-traditional forms: electric guitars are replacing kendo sticks; leathers, bullet bras, and spandex are worn underneath school uniforms; and polite bows are crowded out by militant gestures.

The children of the Urban Samurai have had it with harmony, hierarchy, and duty. Dedicating themselves to the continuation of Japan's economic superiority is no longer considered hip.

But today's alienated youth is far from aimless; it is on a rebellious quest for individuality and creativity — hang the filial piety. One contemplates, however, what impact this tremendous social upheaval will have on the future workers of Japan.

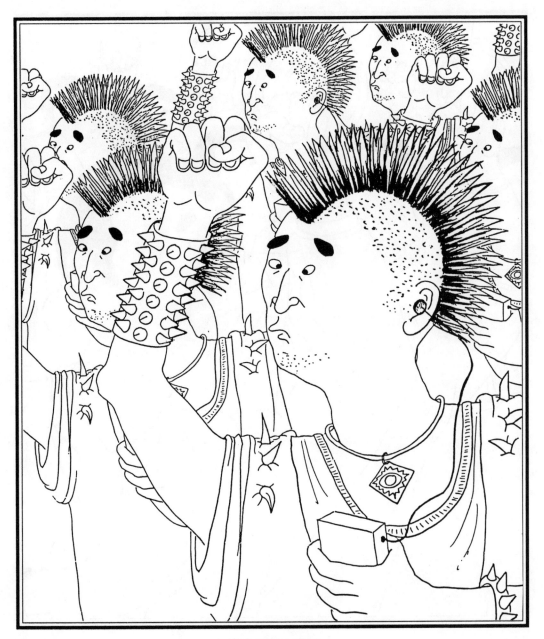

Today's youth

Tomorrow's workers

The Spiritual Quest of the Urban Samurai

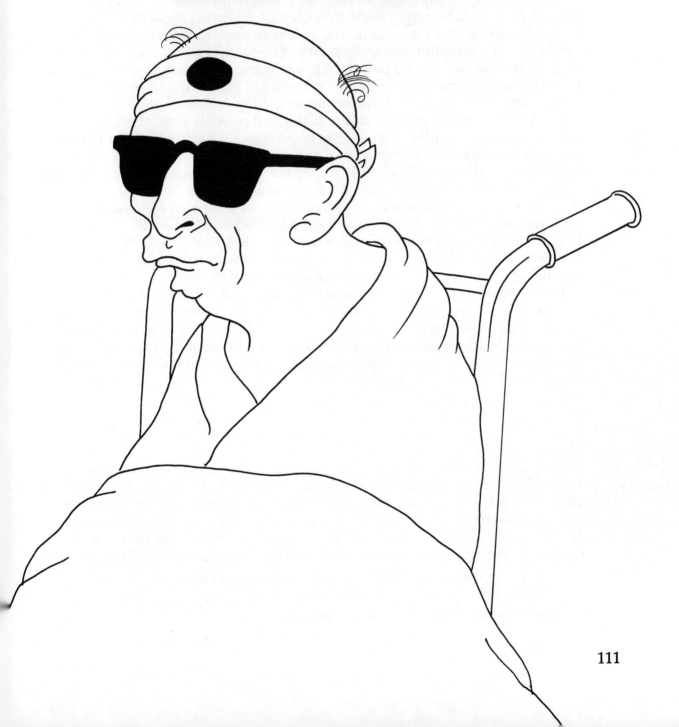

THE ZEN MASTER 900 NUMBER: 1-900-ZEN-4-YOU

The Way of the Urban Samurai

You have studied Japanese tea ceremony, and hang out at the local martial arts discount supply store. You eat with chopsticks and have stopped wearing shoes in your house. You even wear Karate Kid wristbands. But you are still far from understanding the Urban Samurai. *The Way of the Urban Samurai* is not a philosophy, a religion, or a sport. It is the ability to use negation to push oneself to the extremes of experience in order to achieve true wisdom, even if that means forgetting to floss.

The Urban Samurai seeks to attain the highest possible state of mental concentration by shutting out all sense impressions. This is why most Urban Samurai are married. If they were not, most of them would show up at work without their trousers. It is also the reason the Urban Samurai is able to withstand, for hours, sitting on a bus next to a boom box being played at a decibel level equal to that of a rocket-launching at Cape Canaveral, or being on a train so packed he has to leave it in order to change his mind. The true Urban Samurai's higher dimension of consciousness enables him to perceive rap music at 280 decibels as quiet, the crowdedness of the train as emptiness, and the presence of his wife as a layer of ozone.

Every morning, the Urban Samurai looks long and hard at himself in the mirror. Does he see an Urban Samurai? Does he see a man who is absolutely loyal to his boss and has the courage to sacrifice his life in battle, ritual, or at the office? Or does he see a man whose life revolves around paying the mortgage? Does he see a man possessed of an enlightened state of mind and the ability to change the entire economic course of mankind with a single telephone call? Or does he see a man who washes the dishes? Does he see a man whose psychic energies are directed toward the search for the significance of human nature? Or does he see a man who takes the garbage out on his way to work?

Despite years of brutal training as outlined in The Urban Samurai Crash Course, the Urban Samurai on occasion must return to his master for guidance. If he is too busy to attend a weekend refresher training camp in which participants engage in Zen meditation, chanting, and stock market analysis, he can simply dial the convenient Zen master 900 number. The master will present a *koan*, or paradoxical riddle to provide substance for meditation.

> Master: "Well then, my lowly disciple, have you discovered truth and a higher state of consciousness through *The Way of the Urban Samurai*?"

> Urban Samurai: "Yeah, sure, well, uh, y'know . . . "

112

Master: "Very well. We shall see if you have achieved your goal by how you solve this riddle: Is it the flag that is moving, or is it the wind that stirs?"

Urban Samurai: "Uh, hmmmmmmm, uhhhhh. . . .Wait! Master! I've got it!! It is neither! It is neither the flag nor the wind! It's my car!!!"

KASUMI, a professional artist and musician, was married for ten years to an Urban Samurai. Now divorced, she lives with her son in a mid-western city of the U.S.A. Out of respect for her ancestors and hairdresser, she does not reveal her last name.

Photo: Richard Abrams

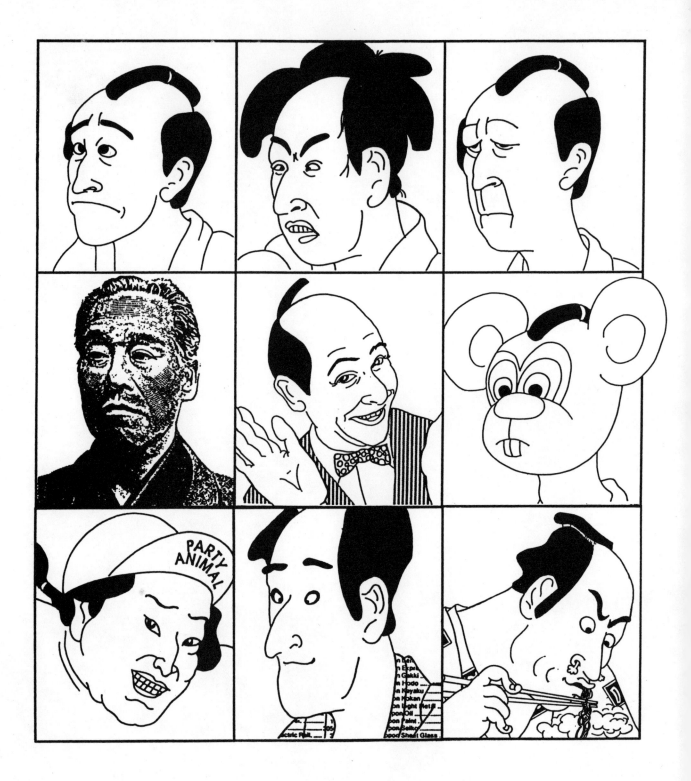